Light relief between grades

Spaß und Entspannung mit leichten Originalstücken für Klavier *Erster Schwierigkeitsgrad*
Plaisir et détente avec des pièces originales simples pour piano *Niveau 1*

Pam Wedgwood

Foreword

Up-Grade! is a collection of new pieces in a wide variety of styles for pianists of any age. This book is designed to be especially useful to students who have passed Grade 1 and would like a break before plunging into the syllabus for Grade 2 – the pieces are pitched roughly at Grade 1 to 2 standard with one or two additional technical challenges, particularly of rhythm in the jazzier numbers.

Whether you're looking for stimulating material to help bridge the gap between grades, or simply need a bit of light relief, I hope you'll enjoy Up-Grade!

I would like to thank Susan Bruce-Payne for many helpful suggestions.

Pam Wedgwood

© 1995 by Faber Music Ltd
First published in 1995 by Faber Music Ltd
Bloomsbury House 74–77 Great Russell Street London WC1B 3DA
Cover design by Stik
Music processed by Wessex Music Services
Printed in England by Caligraving Ltd
All rights reserved

ISBN10: 0-571-51560-6
EAN13: 978-0-571-51560-8

To buy Faber Music publications or to find out about the full range of titles available
please contact your local music retailer or Faber Music sales enquiries:

Faber Music Limited, Burnt Mill, Elizabeth Way, Harlow CM20 2HX
Tel: +44 (0)1279 82 89 82   Fax: +44 (0)1279 82 89 83
sales@fabermusic.com   fabermusic.com

1. Cool Calypso

4

2. The Mad Hatter's Funeral March

Funeral march speed!

3. Homework Blues

4. Chant

Unhurried

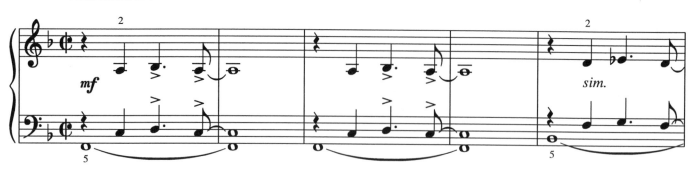

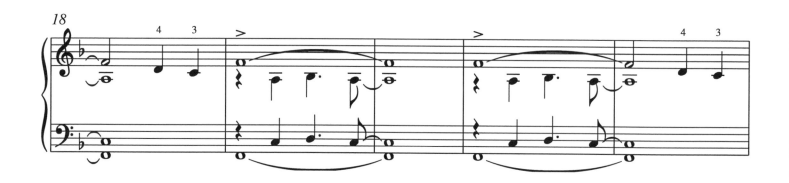

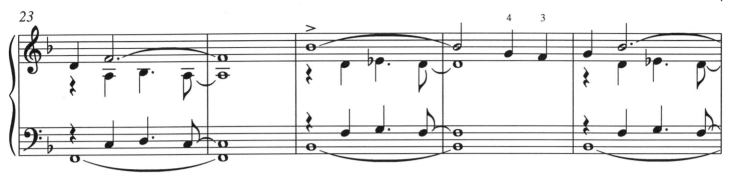

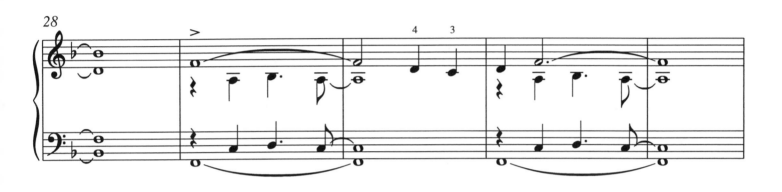

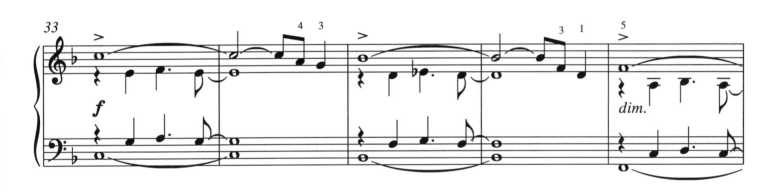

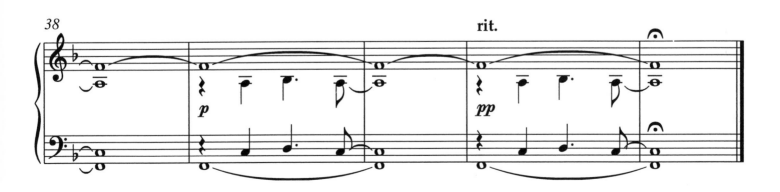

5. Rush Hour Dash

6. The Detective

7. Lazy Days

Unhurried

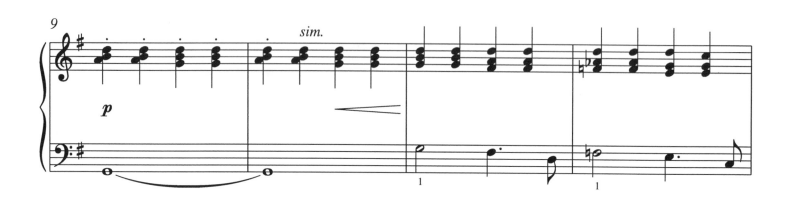

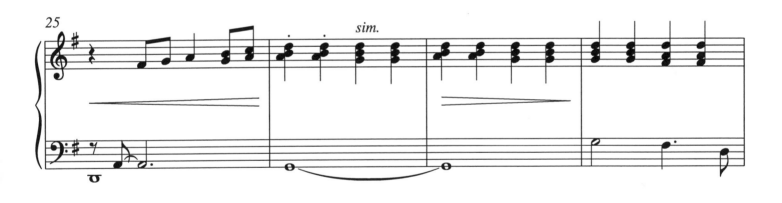

8. The Snake Charmer

Tempo comodo

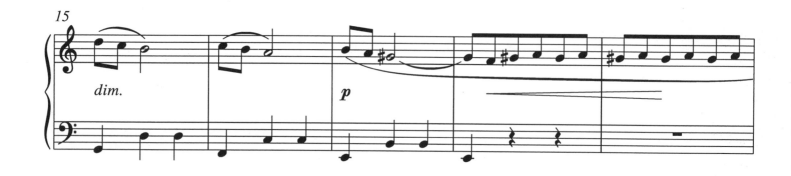

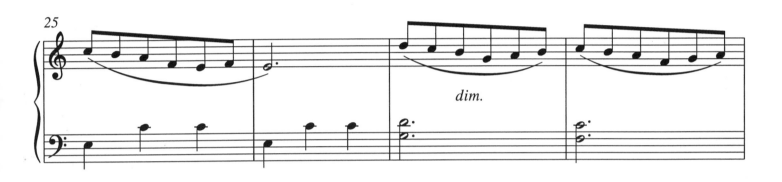

9. Twist and Turn

10. The Cantankerous Camel

Slowish march time

11. Out and About

12. Clowning About

Playfully

13. Masquerade

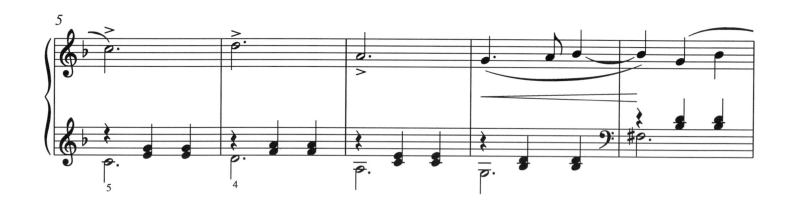

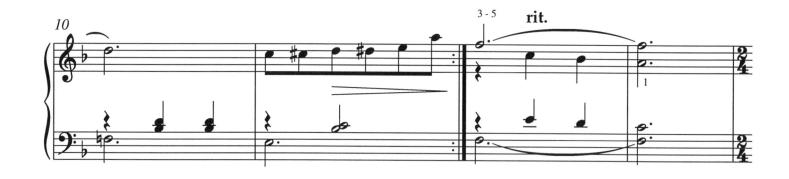

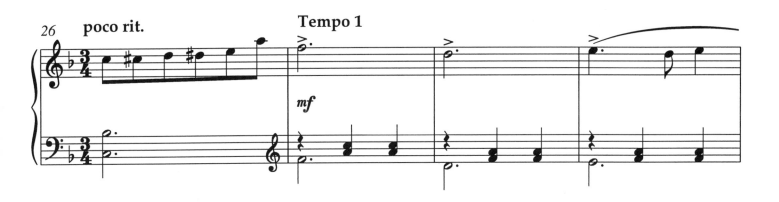

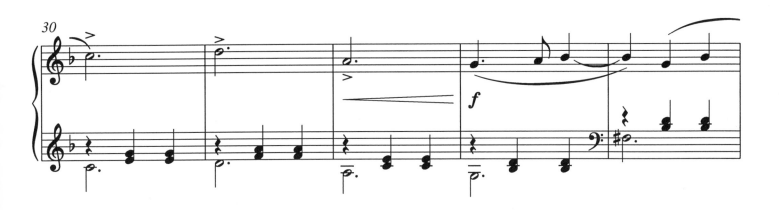

14. Tarantella

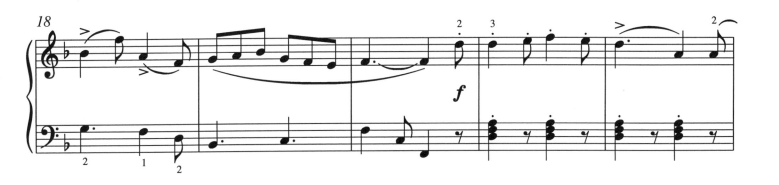

15. Charleston